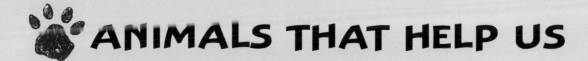

Animals on the Move

Clare Oliver

FRANKLIN WATTS
A Division of Grolier Publishing
NEW YORK • LONDON • HONG KONG • SYDNEY
DANBURY, CONNECTICUT

Picture Credits:

Cover: Panos Pictures (Jean-Léo Dugast)

Interior Pictures: Bruce Coleman pp. 25t (Michael Freeman), 27b (Hans Reinhard), 28b (Hans Reinhard); Ecoscene p. 5t; Eye Ubiquitous p. 26 (L. Fordyce); Sally and Richard Greenhill p. 12; Robert Harding Picture Library pp. 4 (James Green), 13b, 17b (Rolf Richardson), 24 (Christophe Boisvieux), 28t; Houghton's Horses (Kit Houghton) 19; Hutchison Library pp. 11t (Bernard Gerrard), 14 (Jeremy Horner), 15t (Liba Taylor); Impact Photos pp. 7t (Clive Shirley), 9t (Mark Henley), 19 (Moulu/Diapo), 21 (David Reed); Frank Lane Picture Agency pp. 13t (A. Parker); Peter Newark's Western Americana pp. 20t, 20b; Only Horses p. 5b; Oxford Scientific Films pp. 22t (Mike Birkhead), 22b (Belinda Wright), 29t (Mike Hill); Panos Pictures pp. 15b (Alain le Garsmeur), 17t (Jean-Léo Dugast), 23 (Jeremy Horner), 25b (Brian Goddard), 29b (Caroline Penn); Popperfoto p. 27t; Rex Features pp. 8 (Tom Bean), 9b (SIPA/Patrice Lecoq), 16 (Tony White); Still Pictures pp. 6t (Stephen Pern), 6b (Mark Edwards), 7b (Roland Seitre), 10t (William Fautre), 10b (Stephen Pern), 11b (UNEP), 18 (B & C Alexander).

Series editor: Helen Lanz
Series designer: Louise Snowdon
Designer: Sally Boothroyd
Picture research: Sue Mennell

First published in 1999 by Franklin Watts

First American edition 1999 Franklin Watts
A Division of Grolier Publishing
90 Sherman Turnpike
Danbury, CT 06816

Visit Franklin Watts/Children's Press on the Internet at:
http://publishing.grolier.com

A catalog record for this title is available from the Library of Congress.

ISBN: 0-531-14562-X (lib. bdg)   0-531-15405-X (pbk)

Copyright © Franklin Watts 1999
Printed in Malaysia

Contents

From Place to Place

For thousands of years, animals have been used by people for transport. We can travel much farther, and much more quickly, on the back of a horse, donkey, or camel than we can by walking ourselves.

It is easier to transport goods up the steep tracks of the Nepalese mountains by yak than by truck.

Today, cars and trucks are usually a more convenient way of moving both people and goods. But in some parts of the world, modern machinery is too expensive to buy or to run. And sometimes animals are still a better way to move things from place to place.

In the past, horses, mules, donkeys, and camels were not only ridden by people, but were also used as pack animals — they carried heavy goods on their backs. These animals are still used to carry loads today. Other pack animals include elephants, yaks, and llamas.

Draft animals are living machines — they pull objects that we would have difficulty moving on our own.

Oxen are used as draft animals all over the world.

Animals still play an important role in moving things for us, although the types of loads they carry have changed over the years.

In the past, traveling by horseback was a necessity. Today, some people do it just for fun.

In the Saddle

All sorts of animals — from horses and donkeys to elephants and camels — help us by carrying us on their backs.

The Mongolian people of Siberia are nomadic: They move from place to place. They rely on their horses to carry them and their belongings from one resting and trading site to another. Walking, horses can cover 4 mi (7 km) in an hour compared to a person's 3 mi (5 km).

Riding skills are important to Mongol people. They hold a yearly festival to show off their abilities.

Mules and donkeys are both strong animals. They can carry a rider over uneven ground and on narrow paths where a car or truck would not be able to go.

In the sandy lands of West Africa, the Bella Nomads use donkeys as transport.

Camels can carry a rider for 18 hours nonstop, at an average speed of 9 mph (15 kph). In hot, sandy deserts, camels' wide-spreading feet do not sink into the sand like our feet do.

In the jungles of India, people use elephants to trek through the thick undergrowth. Standing 10 ft (3 m) high at the shoulder and weighing 12,125 lb (5,500 kg), Indian elephants are so tall and heavy that very little stops them!

The dromedary was bred for riding. It is faster than its cousin, the Bactrian camel.

Being on elephant-back gives you a good view. These rangers in India are on the lookout for poachers.

A Load to Carry

Pack animals, such as ponies, donkeys, mules, and llamas, are animals that carry a load on their back for their owners. They are often used in craggy mountain areas. Here the roads are often little more than tracks — cars and trucks wouldn't be able to travel along them.

Hikers in Grand Canyon National Park, in the United States, load up a pony with camping equipment.

Ponies and donkeys still work in the steep coastal areas of Spain, Italy, and Greece. They do what they have done for thousands of years: carry a farmer's fruits and vegetables to market. These animals have a more modern use as well. They can help carry heavy camping equipment on long treks, too.

The mule is another important pack animal. Mules are a cross between a horse and a donkey. Mules can put up with very harsh conditions. They keep the hardiness of their donkey fathers but are easy to train like their horse mothers. A big mule can carry about 880 lb (400 kg) — over half its own weight.

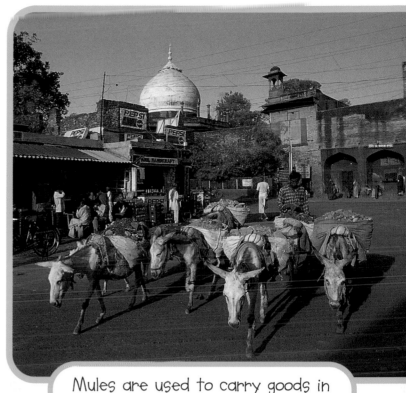

Mules are used to carry goods in the hot and dry climate of India.

High in the mountains of Bolivia, in South America, people mine the rock for salt. They use llamas to carry the heavy loads of salt down the steep paths to the towns below.

The llama is a relative of the camel. Like the camel, llamas can survive on little water and happily eat the scrubby mountain plants. This makes them well suited to the bleak Andes mountains.

A llama can carry a load as heavy as itself about 19 mi (30 km) in one day.

Camel Caravans

The mountains are not the only parts of the world where it is difficult to travel. The barren deserts of Asia and Africa are harsh places. The people who live there often use camels to carry their goods from one place to another.

Camels are very strong. They can travel 40 mi (65 km) a day, carrying up to 400 lb (180 kg).

Camels have special horny pads on the chest and knees. This protects them when they kneel down.

The dromedary stands at just over 6½ ft (2 m) at the shoulder. The Bactrian camel is about 6½ ft (2 m) at the top of its two humps. Camels are trained to kneel down in order to have their loads tied on.

Camels live for up to 40 years (you would be lucky to find a dune buggy that would last for a quarter of that time). Not only that, camels feed themselves, and the water they drink comes free from oases or wells. Buggies need expensive gasoline.

This Bedouin gives his camels water from a well.

Animal Anecdote

Long trains of camels are called caravans. In Roman times, traders used camel caravans to carry silks they bought in China back through the Middle East. They sold the silks to Roman nobles who used them to make fine clothes. The traders' route was known as the Silk Route.

Animal Machines

Long before there were engines, animals were used to power simple machines, by pushing or pulling. This still happens today. The simplest machine that animals pull is the plow.

Water buffalo are often used for heavy farmwork such as plowing.

There are about 78 million animals at work around the world today.

Water buffalo are a common sight in countries such as Vietnam, China, and the Philippines. With their bulky bodies and wide hooves, the animals stand firm in waterlogged land. This makes them the perfect draft animal for the muddy rice fields of Southern Asia.

As well as pulling plows, draft animals are used to operate other farm machines. Donkeys, horses, and oxen can still be seen working corn threshing machines — these machines separate the stalk from the grain. Mills for grinding corn are also sometimes powered by animals.

This donkey is pulling the farmer and his threshing machine over corn to crush out the grain.

In dry, dusty parts of the world, such as India, getting water is a daily struggle. Wells have to be dug deep into the ground, and it takes a lot of power and effort to bring the water to the surface. Oxen or camels are often used to help with this.

These oxen are bringing water to the surface of the well. It is used to water the crops in nearby fields.

Tow Trucks

Other simple machines include carts, carriages, and sleds. Hitched up to one of these, an animal can transport more than one person and pull a larger load than it could carry on its back.

The buffalo's wide hooves help it keep its footing as it strains to pull this heavy load.

Water buffalo weigh about 2,200 lbs (1,000 kg) and measure 6 ft (1.8 m) to the shoulder. Their size and weight give them a lot of strength, making them ideal for pulling heavily laden carts across soft and muddy ground.

In Hungary and Romania, horses are still commonly used to transport goods from one place to another. Donkeys, too, are still widely used throughout Europe, India, and Africa.

These horses in Romania are pulling a load of hay. This will be used to feed them through the winter.

These people from the Mennonite community in Belize use the pulling power of horses to get from place to place.

People in Mennonite and Amish communities still often travel by horse-drawn carts. These people have strong beliefs about how they should live their lives. They live simply, using traditional methods for farming and travel.

Muscle Power

Shire horses, oxen, and elephants are useful to people because of their great strength. Animals like these are used to pull extremely heavy loads, such as rocks from quarries or logs from forests.

Today, tractors are often used instead of horses, but sometimes a team of horses can reach the load more easily.

Some types of horses have been bred especially for heavy draft work. Breeds such as the Suffolk and the Shire are strong and muscular. These horses can weigh more than 1,600 lb (725 kg).

Shire horses are not used as much as they were in the past. However, to this day, the power that can be generated by engines such as tractors is still measured in horsepower.

Oxen are hardy animals that do well in harsh environments where little grows. They are strong and surefooted. Their power and hardiness mean they are often used to pull heavy loads across rough, difficult land.

These oxen in Myanmar (Burma) are being used to pull carts through deep water.

Trained elephants are used in the timber industry to move cut trees and logs. The elephants move the logs from the forests to the river. From there, the water takes the weight, and the logs float downriver to the timber yard.

These elephants in Thailand are trained to use their trunks to lift the logs.

Teamwork

Many draft animals work as part of a team. Combined, they have greater pulling power. Each animal in the team must know its place and must obey the driver's commands in order for the team to work well.

Huskies can pull up to 110 lbs (50 kgs) in weight and survive at −40°F (−40°C).

Arctic people use teams of dogs to pull their sleds across the ice sheets and snowfields. The dogs, such as Siberian Huskies and Alaskan Malamutes, are large, powerful breeds.

A team of six to eight dogs can pull the sled and its driver, who is called the musher, at speeds of 20 mi (32 kph). The older, more experienced dogs run at the front of the team, showing the less experienced dogs what to do.

Animal Anecdote

In 1925 there was an outbreak of diphtheria in the mining town of Nome, Alaska. Emergency supplies pulled by teams of dogs were brought from Anchorage in record time. Now, every March, the Iditarod Trail Dog Sled Race is held to celebrate that journey. The record time for the 1,118-mi race (1,800 km) is just over nine days.

In the past, one of the main ways to travel was by horse and carriage. In most countries, people no longer rely on this type of transport to get around. But in Britain and America, driving horse-drawn carriages is now a sport. The horses travel at tremendous speed — they have to work well as a team and listen carefully to instructions given by the drivers.

Wagon Trail

For some people, traveling by an animal-drawn cart was a way of life.

Between 1836 and 1890, nearly 750,000 people crossed the western frontier of the United States, traveling in horse-drawn wagons. They were on their way to claim land in the West, where they could build new homes and start farms.

Many settlers traveled for six months, covering 2,300 mi (3,700 km).

Life on the move was normal for Native Americans — horses became a necessary part of their lives.

In the late 1800's, Native Americans also used horses to move their belongings. They loaded their teepee, cooking pot, and other possessions onto a palette, called a travois, and dragged it across the ground to the next campsite.

Some people still choose to live in wagons or caravans all the time, like the Roma. The Roma originally came from central and southern Europe, and some traveled as far west as Britain. They traditionally live all their lives in caravans.

The Roma follow old routes in their horse-drawn wagons, staying at villages or towns for a few weeks before moving on.

Each brightly painted wagon contains a whole family of up to ten people.

Roma people depend on their animals to move them from one site to another. They take care of them well.

Down on the Ranch

Cattle ranches are huge farms where people raise cattle to sell. Ranchers need to travel long distances to check the stock or to round up the cows for branding, or marking. They could never cover the ground on foot. So they use horses instead.

Each spring the new calves are rounded up for branding.

Old and new: This cowboy arrived by truck, but he uses a horse to work with the cattle.

A favorite breed for ranchers is the American Quarterhorse. These brave, agile horses face up to the cattle and are able to turn quickly. Nowadays, jeeps are sometimes used instead, but they may frighten the cattle. Also, it is not as easy to track cattle and change direction in a jeep as it is on horseback.

It takes a whole team of ranchers to manage a large herd of cattle.

The trail boss is the leader. Flank riders ride at the sides of the herd to stop the cows from roaming too wide. The drag riders bring up the rear, herding any stragglers.

The drag riders get behind the cattle to drive them across this river in Colombia.

23

Finding and Fetching!

Some animals are used to find and fetch things for us.

Truffles are a very expensive and delicious kind of mushroom. Most truffles grow in France. Because they grow about 1 ft (30 cm) under ground, they are difficult to find. Truffle hunters use pigs or dogs that have been specially trained to pick up the scent of the truffles with their sensitive noses.

Most truffles are found in oak forests.

Coconuts are the tasty fruit of coconut palm trees. These trees grow in tropical countries such as Indonesia and the Philippines. They can grow up to 82 ft (25 m) tall, so picking coconuts can be difficult. In some places, monkeys are trained to harvest the fruits.

Some people don't like to see monkeys used to pick coconuts in this way.

Hawks and falcons are popular breeds to use for falconry.

Falconry is an ancient sport that is still enjoyed all over the world. A falconer trains a bird of prey to hunt animals such as other birds or rabbits.

Falconers wear thick leather gloves to protect their hands from the bird's sharp claws. They carry the bird on the gloved hand for a short time each day so it gets used to being handled. The bird is introduced to lots of sights and sounds until it is tame. After a time, it is released and taught to hunt for its owner.

Animal Messengers

Can you imagine what it would be like to live without telephones, televisions, or computers? How would people know what was going on in the world? In fact, 125 years ago, there were none of these things. People used animals to send information from place to place.

In Yellowstone National Park, visitors see how letters were transported by stagecoach.

Messengers on horseback and stagecoaches were two ways of sending news and letters. At each "stage," or inn, on the way, the horses were changed for fresh, new horses so that the animals did not get too tired.

In 1860, the United States had a famous postal system called the Pony Express. Horse riders carried mail across the country at top speed. But the Pony Express went out of business after just one year, when people were able to send telegrams.

Buffalo Bill, one of the famous characters of the Wild West, started as a Pony Express rider.

Animal Anecdote

Homing pigeons were used in both World Wars for carrying information. A small strip of paper was waxed to make it waterproof and attached to the bird's leg. Because the birds are so small, they were not picked up on the enemy's radar.

Pigeons often flew over 930 mi (1,500 km) to deliver messages. The record flight was made by a U.S. Army Signal Corp's pigeon — 2,300 mi (3,700 km).

On the Move Today

Today, there are all sorts of machines that do the work that animals have traditionally done for us. We travel in cars, jeeps, or snowmobiles, and use tractors on farms. But animals still help us fetch and carry our heavy loads.

Some of these loads have changed in recent years. Donkeys may once have carried coal on their backs, but today they may find that their cargo is a tourist.

In places such as Spain or Britain, tourists take donkey rides along the beach.

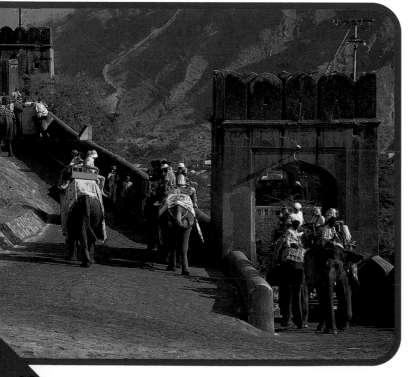

Many people prefer to do their sight-seeing without getting sore feet. When they visit remote temples in the jungles of India, for example, it feels much more exciting to use a traditional form of transport such as an elephant.

Horse-riding has become important to people in another way, too. Racing horses is big business. It provides jobs, gives people an interest, and creates a lot of money. It has become an important sport worldwide.

But all around the world in remote mountain areas, across desert plains or on small farms, animals remain an important method of transport. In these places, animals are still ridden and used to pull carts or power machines as an essential part of everyday life.

These people in Eritrea use donkeys to carry containers heavy with drinking water.

Glossary

agile   able to move quickly.

Bactrian   a camel with two humps.

barren   where nothing grows; a bare area.

draft animal   an animal that pulls a load for its owner.

dromedary   a camel with one hump.

falconry   the sport of training a bird of prey to hunt animals and bring them back to its owner.

goods   objects that are traded. Goods include things such as food and clothes.

hardiness   the ability to survive in difficult conditions.

hitch   to join together with a rope or harness.

pack animal   an animal that carries a load on its back for its owner.

sure-footed   describes an animal or person who is able to place their feet carefully and keep their balance.

Useful Addresses

Alaska Dog Mushers Association
P.O. Box 70622
Fairbanks, AK 99707
http://www.sleddog.org/

A non-profit organization whose aim is to encourage and promote sled dog racing in Alaska.

North American Falconers Association (NAFA)
http://www.n-a-f-a.org/

Group dedicated to the ancient sport of falconry and the conservation of birds of prey.

World of Wings Pigeon Center
2300 N.E. 63rd
Oklahoma City, OK 73111
http://www.worldofwings.org/index2html

Information on famous homing pigeons and their owners, facts on various breeds, and more. Sponsored by the Amerian Homing Pigeon Institute, Inc.

World Wide Fund for Nature Global Network
http://www.panda.org/wwfintlink

The world's largest independent conservation organization. Provides information on endangered species, including "Asian Elephants in the Wild."

Index